RESPONSIBLE CITIZENSHIP

Volunteering

by Kirsten Chang

BLASTOFF! READERS

BELLWETHER MEDIA • MINNEAPOLIS, MN

Blastoff! Readers are carefully developed by literacy experts to build reading stamina and move students toward fluency by combining standards-based content with developmentally appropriate text.

Level 1 provides the most support through repetition of high-frequency words, light text, predictable sentence patterns, and strong visual support.

Level 2 offers early readers a bit more challenge through varied sentences, increased text load, and text-supportive special features.

Level 3 advances early-fluent readers toward fluency through increased text load, less reliance on photos, advancing concepts, longer sentences, and more complex special features.

★ **Blastoff! Universe**

Reading Level

Grade **K**

Grades **1–3**

Grade **4**

This edition first published in 2022 by Bellwether Media, Inc.

No part of this publication may be reproduced in whole or in part without written permission of the publisher. For information regarding permission, write to Bellwether Media, Inc., Attention: Permissions Department, 6012 Blue Circle Drive, Minnetonka, MN 55343.

LC record for Volunteering available at http://lccn.loc.gov/2021016558

Editor: Kieran Downs   Designer: Brittany McIntosh

Printed in the United States of America, North Mankato, MN.

Table of Contents

Helping Others   4

What Is Volunteering?   6

Why Is Volunteering   16
    Important?

Glossary   22

To Learn More   23

Index   24

Helping Others

Kate volunteers
in her free time.
She reads to people
in a nursing home.

What Is Volunteering?

Volunteering is doing a job for free. Anyone can be a volunteer!

Volunteers often work for **organizations**. They help **causes** that they care about.

DONATION

DONATION

9

Lucy helps at the school. She helps students practice reading.

AJ cares for the **environment**. He helps clean up the park.

Max cares about animals. He walks dogs for the **animal shelter**.

Why Is Volunteering Important?

Volunteers do important jobs. They help others in the **community**.

With/Without

important jobs get done

important jobs do not get done

17

We feel good
when we volunteer.
Volunteering helps us
meet new people.

Volunteering makes us better **citizens**!

Why do you think volunteering is important?

Glossary

animal shelter

a place where animals that have nowhere to live can stay

community

certain areas and the people who live there

causes

things that people believe in and support

environment

the land, water, air, plants, and animals around us

citizens

people who are members of a certain town, state, or country

organizations

groups or businesses that form for particular reasons

To Learn More

AT THE LIBRARY

Alexander, Vincent. *Volunteering*. Minneapolis, Minn.: Jump!, 2019.

Taylor, Charlotte. *Volunteers: Making Our Country Better*. New York, N.Y.: Enslow Publishing, 2021.

VanVoorst, Jenny Fretland. *I Am Helpful*. Minneapolis, Minn.: Bellwether Media, 2019.

ON THE WEB

FACTSURFER

Factsurfer.com gives you a safe, fun way to find more information.

1. Go to www.factsurfer.com.

2. Enter "volunteering" into the search box and click 🔍.

3. Select your book cover to see a list of related content.

Index

animal shelter, 14

animals, 14

causes, 8

citizens, 20

clean, 12

community, 16

dogs, 14

environment, 12

help, 16

job, 6, 16

nursing home, 4

organizations, 8

park, 12

people, 4, 18

question, 21

reads, 4, 10

school, 10

students, 10

with/without, 17